Called to Serve

Becoming a Minister of the Gospel

Volume 2

Elder Joel Latimore Jr.

EPIGRAPH

"Moreover it is required in stewards, that a man be found faithful."

— 1 Corinthians 4:2

TABLE OF CONTENTS

- Dedication

- Preface

- Introduction   **Pg 1**

Ch 1 The Weight of Ministerial…   **Pg 8**

Ch 2 The Minister as a Shepherd …   **Pg 26**

Ch 3 Mission Clarity and Moral…   **Pg 47**

Ch 4 Authority, Temptation …   **Pg 71**

Ch 5 Money, Integrity**...**   Pg 93

Ch 6 Loneliness, Pressure …   Pg 117

Ch 7 Accountability, Covering …   Pg 139

Ch 8 Endurance, Finishing Well…   Pg 159

- Epilogue   Pg 184

- Final Charge   Pg 189

- About the Author   Pg 190

DEDICATION

This volume is dedicated to the men and women who answered the call—and remained.

To those who were released into ministry and discovered that authority carries weight, leadership brings loneliness, and obedience often costs more than applause ever could.

To pastors, elders, overseers, and servants who labor faithfully long after the excitement fades—shepherding souls with trembling hands and sober hearts, knowing they must give account before God.

To those who chose restraint over recognition, holiness over popularity, and faithfulness over ambition.

To leaders who remained submitted when independence was easier, pure when compromise was available, and steady when pressure mounted.

To those who endured quietly—misunderstood, criticized, stretched, and tested—yet refused to abandon the trust God placed in their hands.

And to every servant who has learned that the weight of ministry is not a burden to escape, but a trust to carry faithfully before God.

May this volume strengthen your resolve, steady your spirit, and remind you that the weight you carry is seen—and will be rewarded—in the presence of God.

PREFACE

Written for Those Who Carry Responsibility

This volume was not written for those seeking ministry.

It was written for those who are already carrying it.

Volume 1 addressed **formation**—*the shaping of character, discipline, obedience,* and *readiness before God entrusts responsibility.* **Volume 2** begins where formation ends and accountability begins.

Once a minister is released, the questions change.

No longer:

- Am I called?

- Am I ready?

- Am I being prepared?

But rather:

- Am I leading with wisdom?

- Am I handling authority with restraint?

- Am I protecting the people entrusted to me?

- Am I still walking in the fear of the Lord?

Ministry does not become simpler after release—it becomes more demanding. The weight increases. Expectations rise. Scrutiny intensifies. Influence expands. With that influence comes responsibility before God that cannot be taken lightly.

This volume addresses realities many were never taught:

- the burden of leadership

- the temptation that accompanies authority

- the loneliness of responsibility

- the danger of unchecked power

- the necessity of accountability

- the cost of endurance

Scripture makes clear that leaders are judged more strictly. Words spoken from a place of authority carry weight. Decisions made without prayer shape lives. Leadership exercised without humility can fracture the very Body it is meant to protect.

This volume does not seek to discourage ministers—it seeks to steady them.

It calls leaders back to:

- reverence

- restraint

- self-government

- shepherding, not performing

- authority exercised for others, not self

The goal of this volume is not expansion, visibility, or influence.

It is faithfulness.

Not how loudly one speaks—but how carefully.

Not how many follow—but how well they are led.

Not how long one serves—but how one finishes.

If you are carrying responsibility in the Kingdom of God, this volume is written with you in mind. Read it prayerfully. Receive it soberly. Apply it faithfully.

What you carry is not light. What you influence is not temporary. And how you lead will be examined by the God who entrusted it to you.

Carry it carefully.

INTRODUCTION

WHEN RELEASE BECOMES RESPONSIBILITY

There is a moment in every genuine ministry when preparation ends and accountability begins. That moment is not always marked by ceremony, title, or public affirmation. More often, it is marked by expectation—by trust placed quietly, responsibility assumed gradually, and weight felt deeply.

It is the moment when what was formed in private must now be carried in public.

Volume 1 addressed **formation**—*the shaping of character, discipline, obedience,* and *spiritual readiness* before God releases a servant into ministry.

Volume 2 addresses **what follows release:** *the responsibility of carrying authority without corrupting it, leading without abusing it,* and *serving without losing reverence for God or compassion for people.*

Ministry does not grow lighter with time. It grows heavier.

With release comes visibility.

With visibility comes scrutiny.

With authority comes judgment.

Scripture is unambiguous: those who lead God's people will give account—not only for what they preached, but for how they lived; not only for doctrine, but for decisions; not only for intent, but for impact.

This volume is written for those who have discovered that leadership is not sustained by passion alone. It is sustained by **restraint, discernment, humility,** and **endurance.**

It addresses realities many encounter only after they are already serving:

- the burden of making decisions that affect lives

- the loneliness that accompanies responsibility

- the temptation that comes with influence

- the danger of familiarity with holy things

- the fatigue that follows years of giving

This is not a book about ambition.

It is a book about stewardship.

Not about gaining authority—but about governing it.

Not about expanding platforms—but about guarding souls.

Not about surviving criticism—but about remaining faithful under it.

Authority in the Kingdom of God is never granted for self-expression. It is entrusted for *service, protection, correction,* and *care.* When authority is mishandled, people are wounded, faith is shaken, and the name of Christ is dishonored. When authority is carried in the fear of the Lord, the people are strengthened and God is glorified.

This volume calls ministers back to sober leadership—to **self-government** before governing others, to **shepherding** rather than performing, and to **accountability** rather than isolation. It confronts the dangers that arise not before ministry begins, but after it has been established.

The goal of this volume is not to increase confidence, but to deepen caution.

Not to elevate the minister, but to protect the ministry.

Not to impress, but to preserve.

If you are carrying responsibility in the Kingdom
of God, read this volume prayerfully.

What you hold is holy.

What you influence is eternal.

And how you carry what has been entrusted to
you will be examined by the God who gave it.

Lead accordingly.

— Elder Joel Latimore Jr.

CHAPTER 1

THE WEIGHT OF MINISTERIAL AUTHORITY

Ministerial authority is not privilege—it is responsibility under judgment.

When God entrusts a man or woman with authority in His Church, He does not grant them freedom to shape the work according to personality, preference, or ambition. He entrusts them with souls—and with souls comes accountability that reaches beyond time and into eternity.

This is why Scripture does not speak lightly of leadership.

"My brethren, be not many masters, knowing that we shall receive the greater condemnation."
— James 3:1 (KJV)

This warning is not directed at unbelievers.

It is directed at leaders.

Authority in the Kingdom of God places a person under greater scrutiny, not exemption. The minister does not answer only for personal obedience, but for how his leadership shapes the *faith, conduct,* and *stability* of others.

Words spoken in authority carry weight.

Decisions made in leadership alter lives.

Silence in moments requiring courage can
mislead just as much as error spoken aloud.

AUTHORITY IS NOT THE SAME AS ANOINTING

One of the most dangerous misunderstandings in ministry is the assumption that anointing equals approval.

Anointing empowers function.

Authority governs responsibility.

A minister may operate in gifting while mishandling authority. Scripture records individuals who preached, prophesied, and worked miracles, yet were ultimately rejected—not because power was absent, but because obedience and self-government were neglected.

Jesus Himself warned:

"Many will say to me in that day, Lord, Lord, have we not prophesied in thy name… and in thy name done many wonderful works? And then will I profess unto them, I never knew you."

— Matthew 7:22–23

Power does not replace obedience.

Gifting does not excuse carelessness.

Visibility does not cancel accountability.

Authority is not validated by results alone, but by faithfulness, restraint, and reverence.

WHY AUTHORITY INCREASES JUDGMENT

Jesus taught that *"unto whomsoever much is given, of him shall be much required"* **(Luke 12:48).**

Authority multiplies expectation. **The greater the influence, the greater the consequence of misuse.**

A careless leader can wound many at once.

A proud leader can fracture unity.

A compromised leader can normalize sin.

A silent leader can allow deception to spread.

This is why Paul exhorted the elders:

"Take heed therefore unto yourselves, and to all the flock…"

— Acts 20:28

Notice the order:

1. Yourself

2. The flock

Authority exercised without self-examination becomes destructive. Ministers must govern themselves before attempting to govern others.

SELF-GOVERNMENT: THE FIRST TEST OF AUTHORITY

Paul made a sobering confession:

"But I keep under my body, and bring it into subjection: lest that by any means, when I have preached to others, I myself should be a castaway."

— 1 Corinthians 9:27

This is not the language of insecurity—it is the language of reverence.

Self-government includes:

- restraint of speech

- discipline of emotion

- control of desire

- submission to correction

- refusal to act impulsively

**A minister who cannot govern himself will
eventually misuse authority over others.**
Authority does not give permission to indulge—
it demands greater discipline.

AUTHORITY EXISTS FOR STEWARDSHIP, NOT CONTROL

Jesus overturned the world's definition of leadership:

"Ye know that the princes of the Gentiles exercise dominion over them… but it shall not be so among you."

— Matthew 20:25–26

Kingdom authority is not domination.

It is stewardship.

The minister is entrusted with authority to:

- protect the flock

- guide with wisdom

- correct with humility

- serve with compassion

- preserve truth

The moment authority is used to protect ego, silence accountability, or preserve image, it has already drifted from its purpose.

Authority is not a crown—it is a cross.

MINISTERING UNDER THE SHADOW OF CHRIST'S RETURN

The weight of authority increases when viewed through the lens of eternity.

Scripture reminds leaders that Christ's return is not theoretical—it is certain.

"Be ye therefore ready also: for the Son of man cometh at an hour when ye think not."

— Luke 12:40

Ministers will not only answer for what they taught, but for:

- how they lived

- how they led

- how they handled influence

- how they treated God's people

The nearer we are to Christ's return, the greater the need for sober leadership. Casual authority is dangerous in urgent times.

CLOSING CHARGE

Carry authority with fear and humility.

Do not confuse position with permission.

Do not mistake influence for entitlement.

Do not allow familiarity with holy things to dull reverence.

Govern yourself carefully.

Speak deliberately.

Decide prayerfully.

God does not entrust authority lightly, and He does not overlook its misuse. **Those who carry it faithfully protect the people and honor Christ.**

Those who handle it carelessly answer for the damage done.

REFLECTIVE SUMMARY

This chapter establishes that **ministerial authority carries weight, scrutiny,** and **eternal accountability.** Authority is not proof of approval, but a trust that must be governed with humility, discipline, and reverence.

Anointing empowers function, but authority demands stewardship. Ministers are called to govern themselves, serve others faithfully, and lead with eternity in view. Authority exercised without the fear of the Lord endangers both the leader and the flock.

REFLECTIVE QUESTIONS

1. How do I personally define authority in ministry?

2. Do I exercise restraint equal to the influence entrusted to me?

3. How do my words and decisions affect those under my care?

4. Am I governing myself as seriously as I expect others to be governed?

5. How does the reality of Christ's return shape my leadership?

PRAYER

Lord,

Teach me to carry authority with fear and humility. Guard my heart from pride, carelessness, and misuse of influence. Help me to govern myself with discipline, that I may lead others with wisdom and compassion.

Entrust me only with what I can carry faithfully. Correct me quickly, keep me accountable, and let my leadership honor You and protect Your people.

In Jesus' Name, Amen.

CHAPTER 2

THE MINISTER AS A SHEPHERD, NOT A PERFORMER

Ministry is not an assignment to be displayed; it is a trust to be guarded.

Once a minister is released into responsibility, the central danger is no longer immaturity, but misdirection. The call has been confirmed. Authority has been entrusted. Influence has been granted. At this stage, the minister must decide how that authority will be exercised.

Scripture does not present ministers as performers, motivators, or public figures. It presents them as shepherds—men entrusted with the care of living souls who belong to God.

"Feed the flock of God which is among you, taking the oversight thereof..."

— 1 Peter 5:2 (KJV)

A shepherd is measured not by presentation, but by faithful care.

UNDERSTANDING THE BIBLICAL ROLE OF A SHEPHERD

In Scripture, shepherding is not symbolic language—it is functional. A shepherd's responsibilities were well understood:

- feeding the flock

- protecting from danger

- guiding to safe pasture

- tending wounds

- keeping sheep from straying

- remaining present in danger

When God calls a minister a shepherd, He is defining the role, not offering a metaphor.

Jesus identified Himself as the Good Shepherd:

"The good shepherd giveth his life for the sheep. But he that is an hireling… seeth the wolf coming, and leaveth the sheep."

— John 10:11–12

A hireling performs duties for benefit.

A shepherd remains because the sheep matter.

PERFORMANCE VS. SHEPHERDING: A CRITICAL DISTINCTION

Performance-driven ministry focuses on presentation and response. Shepherding-focused ministry centers on responsibility and care.

Performance emphasizes:

- visibility

- eloquence

- emotional reaction

- affirmation

- numbers

Shepherding emphasizes:

- nourishment

- stability

- discernment

- endurance

- protection

A performer asks, "How did they respond?"

A shepherd asks, "Are they growing?"

Performance can produce excitement without maturity.

Shepherding produces strength without spectacle.

FEEDING THE FLOCK: DOCTRINE, BALANCE, AND PATIENCE

Jesus' instruction to Peter was unmistakable:

"Feed my sheep."

— John 21:15–17

Feeding involves more than preaching sermons. It requires consistent instruction, patient repetition, and balanced doctrine. Sheep do not thrive on novelty—they thrive on nourishment.

A shepherd feeds the flock by:

- teaching sound doctrine

- correcting error gently

- reinforcing truth consistently

- applying Scripture practically

- refusing to dilute truth for comfort

When feeding is replaced by entertainment,
believers may feel inspired but remain unstable.

THE RESPONSIBILITY OF SPIRITUAL DISCERNMENT

A shepherd must see what sheep cannot see.

"Grievous wolves shall enter in among you, not sparing the flock."

— Acts 20:29

Discernment is not optional—it is required.

A shepherd must discern:

- unhealthy doctrine

- manipulative influences

- destructive attitudes

- unresolved wounds

- spiritual fatigue

- moral drift

Performance avoids confrontation.

Shepherding confronts to protect.

Correction, when done in humility, is not cruelty—it is care.

AUTHORITY EXPRESSED THROUGH PRESENCE, NOT CONTROL

Biblical authority is not enforced through domination, but demonstrated through faithfulness.

"Neither as being lords over God's heritage, but being ensamples to the flock."

— 1 Peter 5:3

A shepherd's authority is expressed through:

- consistency

- integrity

- example

- accessibility

- restraint

Sheep follow because they trust the shepherd—
not because they are forced.

**When authority becomes controlling,
shepherding has already been abandoned.**

THE EMOTIONAL WEIGHT OF SHEPHERDING

Shepherding is emotionally demanding.

Ministers carry:

- burdens they cannot share publicly

- concerns that do not resolve quickly

- wounds inflicted unintentionally

- criticism from those they serve

Paul described it plainly:

"The care of all the churches."

— 2 Corinthians 11:28

This weight is not incidental—it is part of the calling.

A minister who resents this cost may be functioning as a performer rather than a shepherd.

SHEPHERDING IN LIGHT OF CHRIST'S RETURN

The urgency of Christ's return intensifies the responsibility to shepherd faithfully.

"Blessed is that servant, whom his lord when he cometh shall find so doing."

— Luke 12:43

The question will not be:

- Was your ministry impressive?

- Did people admire you?

But:

- Were the sheep fed?

- Were they protected?

- Were they led in truth?

Ministers serve under the eye of the Chief Shepherd.

CLOSING CHARGE

Reject the temptation to perform.

Do not substitute visibility for vigilance or applause for accountability. Guard your heart against measuring success by response rather than obedience.

Shepherd patiently.

Teach faithfully.

Correct wisely.

Endure quietly.

The flock belongs to God.

You are a steward.

And when the Chief Shepherd appears,
faithfulness—not performance—will be
rewarded.

REFLECTIVE SUMMARY

This chapter establishes **shepherding as the central model for ministry after release.** Ministers are called to feed, protect, and guide God's people with discernment, patience, and integrity.

Performance may attract attention, but shepherding sustains spiritual life.

Authority in ministry is expressed through care, example, and responsibility—not control or spectacle. Those who shepherd faithfully prepare the flock to stand, endure, and remain faithful until Christ's return.

REFLECTIVE QUESTIONS

1. In what ways might performance subtly replace shepherding in my ministry?

2. How intentional am I about feeding the flock with sound, balanced doctrine?

3. Do I avoid correction to preserve comfort or image?

4. How do I carry the emotional weight of shepherding?

5. How does Christ's return shape my priorities as a leader?

PRAYER

Chief Shepherd,

Teach me to shepherd Your people with patience, truth, and humility. Guard me from the temptation to perform or seek approval.

Give me discernment to protect the flock and compassion to care for them faithfully.

Help me to lead in a way that honors You and prepares Your people to stand until You return.

In Jesus' Name, Amen.

CHAPTER 3

MISSION CLARITY AND MORAL RESTRAINT: MOSES AS A PATTERN FOR FAITHFUL LEADERSHIP

One of the clearest indicators of a minister who understands the seriousness of leadership is restraint.

Scripture consistently reveals that when God entrusts a leader with people, He expects that leader to treat those people as a sacred trust—not a personal resource.

**If authority must be governed and people
must be shepherded, then the mission itself
must remain clear.**

Moses stands as one of the strongest biblical
examples of this principle.

Despite leading a nation through crisis,
complaint, rebellion, fear, and fatigue, Scripture
never records Moses exploiting the people
entrusted to him.

There is no record of sexual misconduct.

No manipulation for financial gain.

No emotional dependency upon the people.

No indulgence that compromised the mission.

And because of this, his authority remained trusted—not questioned.

This absence is not incidental.

It is instructional.

Moses understood that he was on assignment— and that assignment required restraint, focus, and the fear of the Lord.

LEADERSHIP AS MISSION, NOT OPPORTUNITY

From the moment Moses encountered God at the burning bush, his leadership was defined as a mission—not a position.

"Come now therefore, and I will send thee unto Pharaoh, that thou mayest bring forth my people…"

— Exodus 3:10 (KJV)

God did not invite Moses to build a following.

He commissioned him to accomplish a deliverance.

Moses understood:

- the people were not his

- the power was not his

- the glory was not his

- the mission was not optional

This clarity governed his conduct.

When leadership becomes opportunity, people become resources.

When leadership remains mission, people remain a responsibility.

MOSES AND THE BOUNDARIES OF LEADERSHIP

Scripture records Moses' frustration, exhaustion, anger, and even failure—but never exploitation.

Moses:

- interceded when judgment was threatened

- pleaded for mercy during rebellion

- bore complaints repeatedly

- endured misunderstanding and criticism

Yet he never:

- blurred moral boundaries

- sought emotional fulfillment from the people

- manipulated resources

- leveraged authority for personal indulgence

Why?

Because Moses understood that misusing the people would dishonor the God who sent him.

"The people are thy people…"

— Exodus 32:7

Moses did not confuse leadership with ownership.

MISSION CLARITY PRODUCES MORAL RESTRAINT

Moses' restraint flowed from clarity. He knew:

- why he was sent

- who sent him

- what was required

- what was at stake

There was no room for indulgence in the wilderness. Delivering a nation required:

- emotional discipline

- moral focus

- spiritual attentiveness

- constant dependence on God

The wilderness demanded sober leadership.

When leaders lose mission clarity, indulgence follows.

When mission remains clear, restraint becomes natural.

MODERN FAILURES AND ANCIENT WISDOM

Many modern ministerial failures do not begin with rebellion—they begin quietly, long before they appear publicly.

- mission is replaced with ambition

- people are treated as emotional or financial support

- boundaries are relaxed

- influence becomes personal

What Moses models is unmistakable:

You cannot shepherd people effectively if you are using them to meet personal needs.

The people are not there to:

- affirm the leader

- soothe insecurities

- satisfy emotional longing

- finance indulgence

They are entrusted to be led, protected, and delivered.

THE COST OF LEADERSHIP WITHOUT INDULGENCE

Moses paid a price for restraint.

He was:

- misunderstood

- unappreciated

- criticized

- burdened

- isolated

Faithfulness often costs more than compromise—but it preserves what compromise would destroy.

Yet Scripture records his intimacy with God:

"The LORD spake unto Moses face to face…"
— Exodus 33:11

God entrusts intimacy to leaders who do not misuse authority.

Restraint preserves clarity.

Clarity preserves intimacy.

Intimacy preserves authority.

DOCTRINAL PRINCIPLE: MISSION CLARITY AS MORAL SAFEGUARD

Definition:

Mission clarity is the understanding that leadership is a divine assignment—not a personal opportunity.

Core Truth:

When a minister understands why he was sent, moral boundaries are maintained internally—not merely enforced externally.

BIBLICAL SUPPORT

- Exodus 3–40

- James 3:1

- Luke 12:48

- 1 Peter 5:2–3

IMPLICATIONS FOR MINISTRY

- Mission clarity prevents moral compromise

- Mission clarity guards financial integrity

- Mission clarity establishes boundaries

- Mission clarity preserves focus and endurance

- Mission clarity protects both leader and people

When mission fades, indulgence grows.

When mission is clear, restraint stands firm.

APPLICATION TO MODERN MINISTRY

Ministers must continually ask:

- Why has God entrusted me with these people?

- Do I see them as responsibility or resource?

- Have I allowed familiarity to blur boundaries?

- Am I guarding the mission—or serving myself?

Moses never forgot the mission—even when it cost him.

CLOSING CHARGE

Guard the mission entrusted to you.

Do not allow personal need, fatigue, loneliness, or pressure to turn God's people into something to be used rather than served.

Maintain clarity.

Protect boundaries.

Fear God.

The assignment is too holy,

the people too precious,

and the time too urgent

for careless leadership.

Guard it carefully.

REFLECTIVE SUMMARY

This chapter presents Moses as a model of **mission-driven leadership marked by restraint, discipline, and reverence.** His clarity safeguarded him from moral compromise and the misuse of authority.

Mission clarity functions as a moral safeguard. It protects both the leader and the people. Ministers who understand why they were sent remain focused, restrained, and faithful— even under pressure.

REFLECTIVE QUESTIONS

1. What specific aspects of Moses' leadership demonstrate mission clarity?

2. Why does Scripture record his failures but not moral exploitation?

3. How does viewing ministry as a mission rather than an opportunity shape leadership behavior?

4. In what ways can ministers unintentionally begin using people?

5. How does mission clarity establish
healthy emotional, financial, and
relational boundaries?

6. How does mission clarity prepare a leader
to stand before Christ?

PRAYER

Lord,

Help me to see clearly why You have entrusted me with those I lead. Guard my heart from ambition, misuse of authority, and blurred boundaries.

Teach me to lead with restraint, discipline, and reverence. Let me treat people as a sacred trust, not a resource.

Keep my mission clear when pressure increases, and do not allow fatigue or desire to distort my purpose.

Let my leadership honor You, my motives remain pure, and help me to finish faithfully.

In Jesus' Name, Amen.

CHAPTER 4

AUTHORITY, TEMPTATION, AND SELF-GOVERNMENT

Authority in ministry does not eliminate temptation—it intensifies it.

If mission clarity guards the leader externally, **self-government must govern the leader internally.**

What is not governed within will eventually surface without.

When a minister is released into leadership, new pressures emerge that were absent during preparation. Influence increases. Access widens. Trust deepens. Expectations multiply. With these changes comes heightened vulnerability that must be met with intentional discipline.

Scripture never presents authority as spiritual immunity. It presents it as increased exposure.

"Let him that thinketh he standeth take heed lest he fall."

— 1 Corinthians 10:12 (KJV)

This warning is especially relevant for those who stand before others.

AUTHORITY CHANGES THE NATURE OF TEMPTATION

Before release, temptation often appears external and obvious. After release, it becomes internal and subtle.

Authority grants access—to people, information, resources, and influence. Each form of access carries responsibility.

At this level, temptation rarely appears as sin—it presents itself as justification.

- exhaustion

- entitlement

- rationalized decisions

- compassion without boundaries

- pressure to maintain image

- the desire for relief

The danger is not only temptation—it is rationalization.

Scripture reveals that spiritual attacks often target leadership:

"Smite the shepherd, and the sheep shall be scattered."

— Zechariah 13:7

A compromised leader does not fall alone. The damage spreads.

THE ILLUSION OF SPIRITUAL MATURITY

One of the most dangerous assumptions in ministry is that maturity reduces the need for discipline.

Scripture teaches the opposite: **discipline is how maturity is preserved.**

Paul, near the end of his ministry, declared:

"I keep under my body, and bring it into subjection."

— 1 Corinthians 9:27

Notice the present tense.

Paul did not outgrow discipline—he deepened it.

When discipline weakens, authority becomes hazardous.

PRIMARY AREAS OF TEMPTATION UNDER AUTHORITY

While temptation varies, three consistent areas of vulnerability emerge after release.

1. EMOTIONAL AND SEXUAL TEMPTATION

Authority places ministers in proximity to vulnerability. People open their lives, wounds, and struggles to those they trust spiritually.

Without self-government, compassion can become emotional dependence—and emotional dependence can become compromise.

Most failures do not begin with desire—they begin with access that was never properly guarded.

Scripture instructs restraint even in appearance:

"Abstain from all appearance of evil."

— 1 Thessalonians 5:22

Self-government establishes boundaries before temptation arises—not after it takes hold.

2. FINANCIAL TEMPTATION AND THE ABUSE OF TRUST

Authority grants access to finances, and financial compromise rarely begins as theft—it begins as justification.

"Feed the flock… not for filthy lucre."
— 1 Peter 5:2

Moses stands again as a model:

"I have not taken one ass from them…"
— Numbers 16:15

Integrity in this area preserves credibility, conscience, and confidence before God.

3. POWER, CONTROL, AND THE FEAR OF LOSING AUTHORITY

Authority can expose insecurity. Leaders may begin to interpret disagreement as rebellion.

When this happens, authority shifts from stewardship to control.

"Neither as being lords over God's heritage."

— 1 Peter 5:3

Control is often rooted in ungoverned fear.

Self-government restrains the impulse to dominate and restores the purpose of authority— to serve, not to silence.

SELF-GOVERNMENT: THE INNER RULE OF THE SPIRIT

Self-government is not personality-based discipline—it is Spirit-governed restraint.

It involves:

- ruling emotions under pressure

- disciplining thoughts before they become actions

- submitting desires to God

- choosing obedience over relief

"He that hath no rule over his own spirit is like a city that is broken down..."

— Proverbs 25:28

Discipline does not restrict a leader—it protects him.

WHY DISCIPLINE MUST INCREASE AS RESPONSIBILITY GROWS

As responsibility expands, discipline must deepen.

Leaders rarely fall suddenly—they drift quietly until collapse becomes inevitable.

"Exercise thyself rather unto godliness."

— 1 Timothy 4:7

Self-government is sustained through:

- prayer that confronts the heart

- accountability that speaks truth

- routines that guard balance

- habits that prevent isolation

What is neglected privately will eventually surface publicly.

Discipline is not maintained by intention alone—it is sustained by structure.

LEADING WITH JUDGMENT IN VIEW

Ministers do not lead merely before people—they lead before Christ.

"For we must all appear before the judgment seat of Christ."

— 2 Corinthians 5:10

This awareness stabilizes the leader.

It restrains indulgence.

It tempers emotion.

It guards decisions.

Self-government is not driven by fear—it is governed by the awareness of God.

CLOSING CHARGE

Do not trust your calling to protect you from temptation.

Authority does not remove weakness—it exposes it.

Govern yourself carefully.

Strengthen discipline.

Guard access.

Welcome accountability.

What is left ungoverned today will demand payment tomorrow.

Lead with restraint.

Serve with humility.

Fear God.

Guard it carefully.

REFLECTIVE SUMMARY

This chapter establishes that **authority increases exposure, and exposure requires self-government.** Temptation becomes more subtle, access becomes more dangerous, and discipline becomes more necessary.

Self-government preserves integrity, protects the flock, and sustains leadership over time. Ministers who govern themselves faithfully can carry authority without compromising holiness or misusing trust.

REFLECTIVE QUESTIONS

1. In what ways has increased responsibility changed the nature of temptation in my life?

2. Which areas of access require stronger boundaries?

3. How intentional am I about self-government as my authority increases?

4. Have I mistaken maturity for reduced need for discipline?

5. How does awareness of Christ's judgment shape my daily decisions?

PRAYER

Lord,

Teach me to govern myself with discipline and humility as I lead others. Guard my heart from temptation, pride, and misuse of authority.

Help me to walk carefully, establish wise boundaries, and remain accountable before You.

Let my private obedience sustain my public responsibility, and keep me faithful to the trust You have placed in my hands.

In Jesus' Name, Amen.

CHAPTER 5

MONEY, INTEGRITY, AND THE STEWARDSHIP OF TRUST

Money is not the only test of ministry, but it is one of the clearest.

Once a minister is released into responsibility, financial pressure increases. Needs expand. Expectations rise. Opportunities multiply.

Nowhere is self-government tested more visibly than in the handling of money, where internal discipline is revealed through external stewardship.

Because money is inseparably connected to trust and influence, its handling becomes a spiritual issue—not merely an administrative one.

Scripture treats financial integrity as a matter of stewardship before God.

"Moreover it is required in stewards, that a man be found faithful."

— 1 Corinthians 4:2 (KJV)

In ministry, money is never just about provision. It is about credibility, conscience, and care for the people. When finances are mishandled, the damage rarely stops with the leader—it spreads into the faith and confidence of the flock.

WHY MONEY TESTS MINISTERS SO SEVERELY

Money tests ministers because it touches multiple areas at once:

- desire and contentment

- fear and security

- identity and success

- control and influence

- justification and compromise

Few leaders fall suddenly into financial scandal. Most drift slowly, beginning with internal reasoning:

- "I deserve this because I sacrifice."

- "The ministry needs it."

- "No one will know."

- "God understands my situation."

What begins as reasoning soon becomes permission.

This is why Scripture repeatedly connects money with the heart.

"For where your treasure is, there will your heart be also."

— Matthew 6:21

Financial compromise often begins in thought long before it appears in action.

THE MINISTER MUST BE ABOVE REPROACH

Paul's qualifications for leadership include financial restraint because credibility matters.

"A bishop then must be blameless… not greedy of filthy lucre."

— 1 Timothy 3:2–3 (KJV)

To be above reproach does not mean perfection. It means living in such a way that accusations lack substance. Even when a leader is innocent, careless financial practices can create suspicion that weakens the ministry.

Wisdom avoids unnecessary exposure.

"Abstain from all appearance of evil."

— 1 Thessalonians 5:22 (KJV)

MOSES: A MODEL OF FINANCIAL CLEANLINESS UNDER AUTHORITY

Moses provides one of the clearest biblical examples of financial integrity under pressure. Leading a nation through hardship invited constant accusation, yet Moses could say before God:

"I have not taken one ass from them, neither have I hurt one of them."

— Numbers 16:15 (KJV)

This statement reveals that Moses governed himself with restraint. He did not treat leadership as entitlement. He did not enrich himself through authority.

And because of this, his leadership remained credible—even under accusation.

Moses understood that the people belonged to God, not to him.

PROVISION VERSUS EXPLOITATION

Scripture affirms that ministers may be supported:

"Even so hath the Lord ordained that they which preach the gospel should live of the gospel."

— 1 Corinthians 9:14 (KJV)

But Scripture also warns that provision can be abused. Paul intentionally limited his financial access to protect the gospel:

"Nevertheless we have not used this power; but suffer all things, lest we should hinder the gospel of Christ."

— 1 Corinthians 9:12 (KJV)

Provision serves the ministry.

Exploitation serves the minister.

Provision is transparent.

Exploitation is manipulative.

The difference lies not merely in policy, but in motive and self-government.

THE PRINCIPLE OF FINANCIAL DISTANCE

DEFINITION

The Principle of Financial Distance is the biblical
practice by which a minister intentionally limits
or removes personal access to financial handling
in order to protect integrity, preserve trust, and
guard the conscience before God and the people.

Distance is not weakness—it is protection.

What is not handled cannot be mishandled.

CORE TRUTH

Spiritual authority does not require financial control. In many cases, distance from money strengthens moral authority rather than weakening leadership.

This principle recognizes that while Scripture affirms ministerial provision, proximity to money creates unnecessary temptation, suspicion, and vulnerability.

BIBLICAL FOUNDATION

- Moses refused personal gain — **Numbers 16:15**

- Paul limited financial rights — **1 Corinthians 9:12**

- Peter warned against financial motive — **1 Peter 5:2**

Restraint is not fear—it is wisdom.

PURPOSE OF FINANCIAL DISTANCE

Financial distance exists to:

1. Protect the minister's conscience

2. Preserve trust with the flock

3. Prevent accusation

4. Maintain role clarity

5. Safeguard the mission

WHAT FINANCIAL DISTANCE IS NOT

This principle does not mean:

- ministers should live without provision

- finances are unimportant

- leaders lack authority

It means authority and access are not the same.

PRACTICAL GUARDRAILS FOR FINANCIAL INTEGRITY

A minister practicing financial distance should:

- separate authority from access

- avoid sole control over accounts

- welcome oversight and documentation

- maintain personal contentment

- refuse to use people as a financial solution

"Godliness with contentment is great gain."

— 1 Timothy 6:6 (KJV)

THE COST OF FINANCIAL COMPROMISE

Financial compromise damages more than reputation. It weakens faith, divides congregations, and brings reproach upon Christ's name.

It teaches people to question what they once trusted.

This is why Scripture demands financial cleanliness in leadership—not because God is concerned with money alone, but because the people's faith must be protected.

CLOSING CHARGE

Handle money as stewardship, not entitlement.

Refuse manipulation.

Refuse secrecy.

Build structures that protect both the flock and the leader.

Maintain a clean conscience before God.

If you cannot say, like Moses, *"I have not taken…"*, then correction is required immediately.

This is not about image.

It is about the fear of the Lord.

Guard it carefully.

REFLECTIVE SUMMARY

This chapter shows that **money is a major test of ministry because it intersects with trust, authority, and motive.** Using Moses and Paul as models, Scripture establishes financial restraint as a mark of faithful leadership.

The Principle of Financial Distance protects integrity, preserves credibility, and safeguards the mission entrusted by God. Financial stewardship is not optional—it is essential to ministerial faithfulness.

REFLECTIVE QUESTIONS

1. Do I view financial provision as stewardship or entitlement?

2. What safeguards protect my ministry from financial compromise?

3. Have I ever used spiritual pressure to influence giving?

4. What does my lifestyle communicate about contentment and integrity?

5. Could I say, with confidence before God, *"I have not taken…"*?

PRAYER

Lord,

Make me a faithful steward. Guard my heart from greed, my hands from misuse, and my ministry from reproach.

Teach me to handle resources with wisdom, restraint, and the fear of the Lord.

Let my life reflect integrity, and keep my leadership clean before You.

In Jesus' Name, Amen.

CHAPTER 6

LONELINESS, PRESSURE, AND THE EMOTIONAL COST OF LEADERSHIP

One of the least discussed realities of ministry is loneliness.

It is not immediately visible, but it is deeply felt.

This is not the loneliness caused by immaturity, withdrawal, or broken relationships—it is the loneliness that comes from responsibility. As authority increases, relational symmetry decreases. Leaders cannot speak freely in every space, share every burden publicly, or process every decision aloud. This silence is not deception; it is discretion.

Faithful stewardship is not only measured in how a leader handles resources, but in how he carries the weight those responsibilities create.

This is not the absence of people—it is the weight of being responsible for them.

Scripture does not hide this cost. It records leaders who carried responsibility with few peers, limited relief, and constant pressure—yet remained faithful.

"And I was left alone; and I saw this great vision…"

— **Daniel 10:8 (KJV)**

Leadership often requires standing alone—not because others are absent, but because responsibility cannot be shared equally.

WHY LEADERSHIP PRODUCES LONELINESS

Loneliness in ministry is not primarily social; it is structural. As responsibility increases, the nature of relationships changes. Decisions carry greater consequence. Words must be weighed carefully. Transparency must be selective, and vulnerability must be exercised with wisdom.

A leader often protects others from the weight he carries. This protection, while necessary, creates emotional distance—even in healthy environments.

Jesus Himself experienced this reality:

"Could ye not watch with me one hour?"

— Matthew 26:40 (KJV)

The failure of others to carry the weight did not negate His mission, but it did increase His solitude.

THE PRESSURE OF BEING THE ONE WHO MUST DECIDE

Leadership concentrates pressure. While many may advise, pray, and contribute, someone must ultimately decide—and live with the outcome.

Pressure in ministry often arises from unresolved conflict, competing expectations, the emotional needs of others, criticism without context, and decisions made without full information.

And often, it must be carried without full explanation.

This pressure is not episodic; it is cumulative.

It follows the leader beyond the moment and into the mind.

Paul described it plainly:

"That which cometh upon me daily, the care of all the churches."

— 2 Corinthians 11:28 (KJV)

This kind of pressure does not disappear after prayer alone. It must be continually managed, processed, and brought before God.

THE EMOTIONAL BURDEN OF CARING FOR SOULS

Shepherding requires emotional investment. Ministers walk with people through grief and loss, moral failure, marital strain, spiritual confusion, and disappointment with God. This exposure is sacred, but it is also costly.

The same openness that allows people to be helped also makes the leader vulnerable.

Leaders must learn to care deeply without absorbing destructively. Scripture cautions:

"Keep thy heart with all diligence; for out of it are the issues of life."

— Proverbs 4:23 (KJV)

Guarding the heart does not mean withholding compassion. It means governing emotional intake so that care remains sustainable over time.

WHY SOME LEADERS BURN OUT QUIETLY

Burnout rarely begins with rebellion—it begins with pressure that is carried but never released.

When emotional strain is ignored, it often surfaces later as numbness, irritability, withdrawal, cynicism, or fatigue disguised as faithfulness.

Moses reached such a moment when the burden exceeded his capacity:

"I am not able to bear all this people alone."

— Numbers 11:14 (KJV)

God's response was not rebuke, but shared support. This teaches that acknowledging limits is not failure—it is wisdom.

HEALTHY SOLITUDE VERSUS HARMFUL ISOLATION

Scripture makes a clear distinction between solitude chosen for renewal and isolation created by fear or despair.

Jesus withdrew to pray and was strengthened.

Elijah withdrew in despair and became discouraged.

Solitude restores perspective, deepens prayer, and renews strength. Isolation magnifies discouragement, distorts perception, and weakens judgment.

What begins as protection can become separation if not governed carefully.

Without awareness, necessary distance can become unnecessary isolation.

Leaders must discern when to withdraw for God—and when to reach out for help.

"Two are better than one…"
— Ecclesiastes 4:9 (KJV)

Even strong leaders need wise counsel.

PROCESSING PRESSURE WITHOUT TRANSFERRING IT

One of the marks of mature leadership is the ability to process pressure without passing it down.

Immature leaders often discharge stress through harsh speech, impulsive decisions, or emotional volatility. Mature leaders pray before responding, seek counsel privately, regulate tone and timing, and protect the people from unnecessary weight.

They refuse to make permanent decisions under temporary pressure or emotional strain.

Jesus did not vent His pressure to the disciples. Scripture says:

"He poured out his soul unto death…"

— Isaiah 53:12 (KJV)

Leaders must learn where—and to whom—to pour out their souls.

SUSTAINING THE INNER LIFE OF THE MINISTER

Longevity in ministry depends on intentional care of the inner life. Public ministry can never replace private renewal.

This care includes:

- disciplined prayer beyond public ministry

- honest self-examination

- spiritual friendships with peers

- rest without guilt

- permission to be human before God

"He restoreth my soul."

— **Psalm 23:3 (KJV)**

Restoration is not weakness—it is maintenance.

CLOSING CHARGE

Do not ignore the emotional cost of leadership.

Loneliness does not mean failure.

Pressure does not mean disobedience.

But unmanaged strain will eventually surface in unhealthy ways.

Guard your heart.

Seek counsel.

Withdraw wisely.

Pour out your soul before God.

The weight you carry is not a mistake—it is part of the assignment.

The One who called you understands the weight you carry, and He remains near to those who lead faithfully under pressure.

Carry it faithfully.

REFLECTIVE SUMMARY

This chapter addresses the realities of loneliness and emotional pressure in ministry. Leadership concentrates responsibility, limits transparency, and creates emotional strain that must be managed with wisdom.

Sustainable ministry requires intentional care of the inner life, healthy processing of pressure, and discernment between restorative solitude and harmful isolation. Leaders who acknowledge these realities are better equipped to endure faithfully.

REFLECTIVE QUESTIONS

1. How has increased responsibility affected my emotional life?

2. Do I distinguish between healthy solitude and harmful isolation?

3. Where do I process pressure safely and prayerfully?

4. Have I allowed unprocessed strain to affect my leadership tone or decisions?

5. What practices consistently restore my soul?

PRAYER

Lord,

You know the weight I carry and the silence that often accompanies responsibility. Restore my soul and guard my heart, and teach me to process pressure wisely.

Help me to lead with compassion without becoming depleted, and to seek You as my refuge.

Sustain me for the long journey, and keep me faithful under the weight You have entrusted to me.

In Jesus' Name, Amen.

CHAPTER 7

ACCOUNTABILITY, COVERING, AND THE DANGER OF ISOLATION

One of the most dangerous myths in ministry is that spiritual authority reduces the need for accountability—when in reality, it increases it.

Scripture teaches the opposite: the greater the authority, the greater the need for covering, counsel, and correction.

The same pressures that create emotional strain also create the need for accountability—because what is carried alone is rarely processed correctly. And what is not processed correctly is rarely led correctly.

Isolation does not usually begin as rebellion. It begins as independence justified by experience, position, or fatigue. Leaders who once welcomed counsel may gradually limit voices and distance themselves from those who can speak truthfully into their lives.

It begins quietly, often unnoticed by the leader himself. It rarely feels dangerous in its early stages.

What begins as protection of focus can quietly become protection of pride.

Scripture warns plainly:

"Pride goeth before destruction, and an haughty spirit before a fall."

— Proverbs 16:18 (KJV)

Accountability is not a threat to leadership—it is a safeguard for it.

AUTHORITY DOES NOT CANCEL SUBMISSION

No leader in Scripture functioned without accountability to God and to others. Even Moses, the most authoritative leader in Israel, received correction, instruction, and delegation through Jethro. David, though king, submitted to prophets. Paul, though apostle, remained accountable to the body and to his fellow laborers.

Authority in the Kingdom of God does not remove submission—it redefines it.

"Submitting yourselves one to another in the fear of God."

— Ephesians 5:21 (KJV)

Submission is not weakness—it is alignment.

It keeps authority from drifting into independence.

No one graduates from submission in the Kingdom of God.

Leaders who resist accountability often confuse submission with control and counsel with challenge. Scripture never supports that confusion.

THE ROLE OF SPIRITUAL COVERING

Covering is not domination.

Covering is protection, oversight, and spiritual alignment.

A true covering does not exist to silence a leader, but to preserve them. It provides:

- perspective when pressure distorts judgment

- correction when blind spots emerge

- support when isolation increases

- restraint when authority is tempted toward excess

Paul described this protective function when he spoke of watching over souls as those who must give account:

"They watch for your souls…"

— Hebrews 13:17 (KJV)

A leader without covering may still function— but they function unprotected, and eventually, unchecked.

WHY ISOLATION IS ESPECIALLY DANGEROUS FOR LEADERS

Isolation removes friction—and without friction, there is nothing to confront error or challenge perception.

When a leader limits access, restricts accountability, or refuses correction, warning signs may go unnoticed until damage is already done. Isolation allows internal reasoning to go unchallenged and emotional strain to remain unprocessed.

Scripture records that even strong leaders were vulnerable when isolated. Elijah's despair deepened when he withdrew without counsel.

His perception became distorted until God intervened.

Isolation does not usually announce itself as danger. It often disguises itself as privacy, efficiency, or protection of vision.

PEER ACCOUNTABILITY AND EQUAL VOICES

Healthy accountability does not come only from those under authority, but from peers who understand the weight of leadership.

Paul traveled with companions. He reasoned with fellow apostles. He submitted his gospel to others "lest by any means" he run in vain. This demonstrates that maturity seeks confirmation, not insulation.

Peers do not replace authority—they reinforce clarity.

They prevent the leader from becoming the only voice they hear.

Leaders need voices who:

- are not impressed by position

- are not dependent on access

- are not intimidated by authority

- are committed to truth over comfort

Such relationships protect leaders from self-deception.

CORRECTION AS A GIFT, NOT AN ATTACK

Correction is one of the clearest tests of spiritual maturity. Leaders who view correction as dishonor often resist the very process God uses to preserve them.

Scripture says:

"Let the righteous smite me; it shall be a kindness."

— Psalm 141:5 (KJV)

Correction offered in humility is not an attempt to diminish authority, but to refine it.

Correction received properly preserves both the leader and the people they lead.

Leaders who receive correction wisely strengthen their credibility. Those who reject it weaken their witness.

Correction resisted becomes correction delayed—and correction delayed often becomes judgment enforced.

THE ACCOUNTABILITY OF STANDING BEFORE CHRIST

Ultimately, all human accountability points toward divine accountability.

"For we must all appear before the judgment seat of Christ."

— 2 Corinthians 5:10 (KJV)

No title, office, or experience exempts a leader from this reality. Remembering future judgment tempers present authority.

They do not merely lead for results—they lead for accountability.

They remember that authority will be examined, not assumed.

Leaders who lead with eternity in view remain *teachable, careful,* and *restrained.*

CLOSING CHARGE

Do not lead alone.

Seek covering.

Welcome counsel.

Remain teachable.

Refuse isolation disguised as independence.

Authority without accountability becomes dangerous.

Leadership without correction becomes distorted.

Power without submission becomes destructive.

God protects leaders who remain under authority.

Protection remains where submission remains.

Remain under it.

REFLECTIVE SUMMARY

This chapter has examined the necessity of accountability, spiritual covering, and peer counsel in ministry. Scripture consistently teaches that authority increases the need for submission, not independence.

Isolation exposes leaders to blind spots, distorted judgment, and unchallenged reasoning. Accountability protects integrity, preserves humility, and sustains leadership over time.

Leaders who remain teachable and covered are better equipped to endure faithfully.

REFLECTIVE QUESTIONS

1. Who has permission to speak truthfully into my life without fear of reprisal?

2. Have I confused authority with independence in any area of leadership?

3. How do I respond internally when corrected or challenged?

4. Do I maintain relationships with peers who understand the weight of leadership?

5. How does the reality of standing before Christ shape my openness to accountability?

PRAYER

Lord,

Keep me humble, teachable, and submitted before You. Protect me from isolation, pride, and self-deception.

Place wise voices around me who will speak truth in love and guard my leadership from error.

Help me to lead under authority as I lead with authority, remembering that I will give account before You.

Preserve my integrity and keep my heart aligned with Your will.

In Jesus' Name, Amen.

CHAPTER 8

ENDURANCE, FINISHING WELL, AND FAITHFUL COMPLETION

The measure of ministry is not how it begins—it is how it finishes.

And finishing well is not accidental—it is the result of everything that has been guarded, governed, and submitted along the way.

Many begin with sincerity, zeal, and clear calling—but not all finish with faithfulness. Scripture consistently reveals that beginning well does not guarantee finishing well.

Endurance is the final and most revealing test of leadership.

Everything addressed in this volume—authority, shepherding, restraint, self-government, integrity, emotional endurance, and accountability—finds its ultimate purpose in this: remaining faithful over time.

WHY FINISHING WELL MATTERS

Scripture does not celebrate strong beginnings alone. It honors faithful completion.

"Be thou faithful unto death, and I will give thee a crown of life."

— **Revelation 2:10 (KJV)**

Finishing well means:

- maintaining integrity over time

- preserving character under pressure

- continuing in truth despite fatigue

- remaining accountable when influence increases

- enduring when recognition fades

A strong start may gain attention—but a faithful finish earns reward.

THE DANGER OF MID-JOURNEY FAILURE

Many failures in ministry do not occur at the beginning—they occur after years of service.

Why?

Because:

- familiarity replaces reverence

- routine replaces dependence

- experience replaces vigilance

- success reduces caution

What was once guarded becomes assumed. What was once intentional becomes automatic.

When vigilance decreases, vulnerability increases.

And what is no longer guarded eventually becomes vulnerable.

Scripture provides sobering examples of leaders who began well but faltered later—not because they lacked calling, but because they ceased guarding what had been entrusted to them.

ENDURANCE IS NOT PASSIVE—IT IS INTENTIONAL

Endurance is not merely surviving time. It is actively maintaining alignment with God over time.

Paul described his own pursuit:

"I have fought a good fight, I have finished my course, I have kept the faith."

— 2 Timothy 4:7 (KJV)

Notice the language:

- fought

- finished

- kept

Endurance requires engagement, not drift.

Drift is the enemy of endurance.

A leader who intends to finish well must remain:

- watchful in private life

- disciplined in personal conduct

- accountable in relationships

- faithful in doctrine

- sensitive to the Holy Spirit

GUARDING WHAT HAS BEEN ENTRUSTED

Paul instructed Timothy:

"That good thing which was committed unto thee keep..."

— 2 Timothy 1:14 (KJV)

Ministry is not self-created—it is entrusted.

And what is entrusted must be guarded:

- guard your doctrine

- guard your integrity

- guard your relationships

- guard your motives

- guard your private life

What is not guarded will eventually be lost.

THE ROLE OF FATIGUE IN LONG-TERM MINISTRY

Fatigue is one of the greatest threats to endurance.

Not always physical fatigue—but:

- emotional fatigue

- spiritual fatigue

- decision fatigue

- relational fatigue

Fatigue does not always announce itself.

It often disguises itself as normal, until its effects become spiritual.

It often appears as:

- reduced sensitivity

- shortened patience

- diminished prayer

- quiet compromise

When fatigue is ignored, discernment weakens.

Scripture warns:

"Let us not be weary in well doing..."

— Galatians 6:9 (KJV)

This is not merely encouragement—it is instruction.

CONSISTENCY OVER INTENSITY

Many leaders rely on intensity to sustain ministry—but intensity fades.

What sustains leadership is consistency.

Daily obedience.
Daily discipline.
Daily submission.

Consistency builds what intensity cannot sustain.

What is done daily determines what is sustained long-term.

Jesus' life was not marked by bursts of effort—but by steady obedience to the will of the Father.

HUMILITY AS THE KEY TO FINISHING WELL

Pride is one of the greatest threats to endurance.

A leader who stops listening, stops receiving correction, or begins to rely on past success rather than present obedience places himself at risk.

Scripture reminds us:

"God resisteth the proud, but giveth grace unto the humble."

— James 4:6 (KJV)

Grace sustains those who remain humble.

Humility keeps the leader in a position where grace can continue to flow.

A leader who finishes well is not one who never faced pressure—but one who remained submitted through it.

KEEPING ETERNITY IN VIEW

Endurance is strengthened when eternity remains the focus.

Leaders who remember that they will stand before Christ live differently than those who focus only on present results.

"For we walk by faith, not by sight."

— 2 Corinthians 5:7 (KJV)

Eternal awareness produces present discipline.

It reminds the leader that every decision is moving toward a final account.

It keeps:

- motives pure

- decisions careful

- leadership sober

FINISHING WITH INTEGRITY

To finish well is to arrive at the end of one's ministry with:

- a clean conscience

- a faithful testimony

- a preserved calling

- a guarded life

Not perfect—but faithful.

Not flawless—but consistent.

God does not require perfection—He requires faithfulness.

CLOSING CHARGE

Do not measure your ministry by how it begins.

Measure it by how it is sustained.

Guard what God has entrusted to you.

Remain disciplined when no one is watching.

Stay accountable when influence increases.

Endure when the weight becomes heavy.

The goal is not to start strong—it is to finish faithful.

What you carry matters.

How you carry it matters.

How you finish will be examined by God.

And what you preserved will matter more than what you built.

Finish well.

Finish faithfully.

REFLECTIVE SUMMARY

This chapter emphasizes that endurance is the final measure of ministry. Faithfulness over time requires discipline, humility, vigilance, and intentional alignment with God.

Leaders who finish well are those who consistently guard what has been entrusted, remain accountable, and endure through fatigue, pressure, and time.

REFLECTIVE QUESTIONS

1. Am I more focused on starting strong or finishing faithfully?

2. What areas of my life require renewed vigilance?

3. How do I respond to fatigue in ministry?

4. Have I allowed familiarity to reduce reverence?

5. What practices help me maintain consistency over time?

PRAYER

Lord,

Help me to remain faithful over time. Guard my heart from pride, fatigue, and carelessness.

Strengthen me to endure with integrity, to remain disciplined in private, and to walk humbly before You.

Teach me to guard what You have entrusted to me, and help me to finish well.

In Jesus' Name, Amen.

EPILOGUE

THE WEIGHT YOU CARRY

There is a difference between knowing what ministry requires and carrying what ministry demands.

This book has addressed responsibility, authority, restraint, integrity, endurance, and accountability. These are not abstract principles. They are realities that shape the life of every man or woman entrusted with leadership in the Kingdom of God.

But beyond every principle is a simple truth:

What you carry is not light.

It was given by God.

It is sustained by God.

And it will be examined by God.

You will not answer for another man's calling.

You will not stand before God for another person's assignment.

But you will answer for what was placed in your hands.

There will be days when the weight feels manageable.

There will be days when it does not.

There will be moments of clarity—and moments of pressure.

Moments of strength—and moments of fatigue.

But none of these moments change the responsibility.

The call of God is not seasonal. It is lifelong.

You have been entrusted with people, with truth,
with influence, and with responsibility that
cannot be taken lightly.

Guard it.

Not occasionally—but consistently.

Not when convenient—but at all times.

You have been warned.

You have been instructed.

You have been reminded.

Now you must walk.

Walk carefully.

Walk humbly.

Walk faithfully.

Because in the end, it will not matter how visible your ministry was.

It will matter how faithful you were with what God gave you.

And when that day comes—

May you be found faithful.

FINAL CHARGE

Guard what has been entrusted to you.

Govern yourself before you lead others.

Remain accountable.

Endure the weight.

And finish faithfully.

ABOUT THE AUTHOR

Elder Joel Latimore Jr. is an ordained pastor, Bible teacher, and author with over forty years of ministry experience. His teaching reflects a life shaped by Scripture, discipline, and the work of the Holy Ghost.

He is committed to strengthening believers and equipping ministers to walk in faithfulness, accountability, and obedience to the call of God. His ministry is marked by a clear emphasis on spiritual maturity, sound doctrine, and the practical application of biblical truth in everyday life.

In addition to his teaching ministry, he has devoted years to mentoring and ministering to individuals in challenging environments, including outreach to incarcerated youth.

Through this work, he has consistently emphasized transformation through truth, personal responsibility, and the power of a life governed by the Spirit.

His writing confronts, instructs, and encourages—calling readers beyond surface-level belief into disciplined, Spirit-led living. He carries a burden to see leaders walk in integrity, remain accountable, and endure faithfully in the assignments God has entrusted to them.

Elder Latimore's message is rooted in one central conviction:

That true authority in the Kingdom of God is not demonstrated through position or visibility, but through a life that is governed, submitted, and faithful before God.